Adopted Like Me

Written by
Jeffrey R. LaCure, M.S.W., LICSW

Illustrated by
Michael Edwin Williams

**Dedicated to all the wonderful children who are ADOPTED LIKE ME.
"You are not special because of adoption, but because you are."**

A special thanks to my mother and father for sharing in the excitement that each new day offers. Thanks to my brother for reminding me that each person finds their own way. For my two sons, thank you for constantly reminding me what success is all about. And to Karen, like a fresh morning dew, you make it all possible.

Jeffrey R. LaCure

I would like to dedicate this book to my step-mother Helen; to my wife Debbie for her patience; and to my children through marriage, Melissa and Billy, all of whom have enriched my life.

Michael Edwin Williams

ADOPTED LIKE ME

**Written by Jeffrey R. LaCure
Illustrated by Michael Edwin Williams**

Published by The Adoption Advocate Publishing Company
140 David Road, Franklin, Massachusetts 02038

Text Copyright © 1992 by Jeffrey R. LaCure
Illustrations Copyright © 1992 by Michael Edwin Williams.
    All rights reserved.

Book design, typography and electronic pagination by Arrow Graphics, Inc.
    Watertown, Massachusetts

Printed in the United States of America

ISBN 0-9635717-0-2

There once was a couple who tried for years to have a family;
They did all they could but a baby was just not to be.

They loved one another dearly, yet, had much more love to share;
They were ready to become parents, ready for a baby to care.

Mary then said to her husband Ted E.;
It's time we make an appointment with the adoption agency.

The agency is a place where many families get their start;
Where adoption builds families because there's love in their hearts.

There once was a couple who were happy together;
They made each other laugh, even in the most unpleasant of weather.

Summer was ending, and college was in the fall;
They believed they were forever, they thought they could have it all.

Yes, it was true, they needed each other;
However, unexpectedly and unplanned—she was going to be a mother.

He did not know if he was happy or sad;
But one thing for sure, he was not ready to be a dad.

They held each other close and cried through the night;
It was their hardest decision, they wanted to do what was right.

After weeks of discussion with friends and family;
They knew they were not ready for the commitment parenting would be.

They placed their baby for adoption with much sadness and sorrow;
Yet, were rewarded in knowing, they gave their baby a new chance for tomorrow.

They gave their baby letters, pictures and some family history;
And their love to take with him as he joined his new family.

Mary and Ted E. soon got the call;
Their baby was here, and oh so small.

They picked him up gently, they were as happy as could be;
Their prayers had been answered, and his name was Ben E.

To bring Ben E. home, they traveled by plane;
What's that you say? His address? It's 2 Gilford Goose Lane.

His room was bright blue with a crib and a swing;
His grandparents were so excited, they wanted to give him everything.

Soon the time passed and Ben E. was 4;
Much to his parents' surprise, he began to ask more.

"Daddy" he said, "I might like a baby sister,
Would she be adopted, and where would we get her?"

Now Mary and Ted E. had always hoped it would be;
That they would have another child to add to their adoptive family.

Talking with the agency, it would take a year or two;
"Ben E." they said, "It's worth the wait to have someone like you."

More summers passed and Ben E. grew and grew;
Time moved quickly, it was his third year of school.

School was fun, especially recess;
He wasn't quite sure which subject he liked best.

Day after day the school year moved on;
When one afternoon he said to his mom,

"Mom, I haven't met anyone who said they're adopted,
I've asked Minnie, Barbara, Brian and Ed."

"Ben E." she said, "I've always known since you were two;
That you would want to meet someone who's adopted like you."

"Sometimes children who are adopted aren't sure what to say;
Their friends might be supportive, or they might not want to play."

"Mom" he said, "I wonder what people think because I don't look like you;
Do I tell them I'm adopted? I'm not sure what I should do."

"Ben E." she said, "some families are created by adoption, some by birth;
Both are very loving, and both have their worth."

"Mom" he asked, "Do my birth parents think about me?
Do they wonder what I'm doing? Do they wonder where I might be?"

Now these are questions all adopted children ponder;
If you have a question, ask it, it's o.k. to wonder.

His mother responded as the sun kissed her hair;
"Your birth parents miss you, your birth parents care."

"Daddy and I owe them both so much, it's true;
For without them, we wouldn't have you!"

When Ben E. went to school just the very next day;
There was a new boy in class who lived down the way.

The teacher Ms. Carnera showed him to his desk;
It was right next to Ben E.'s, and his desk was such a mess.

Soon the two got to talking, his name was Mikey,
Ben E. thought to himself, he seems pretty nice to me.

Then the bell rang, signaling the time for lunch;
They were building a friendship, they liked each other a bunch.

After school was over they walked home together;
Mikey said "can I share something with you? Something that's forever?"

"My parents adopted me when I was just three;
I thought I would share this with you, my friend, Ben E."

Ben E. smiled and replied "can I share something with you?
Guess what? You might not believe this, but I'm adopted too."

They asked each other questions, they asked quite a few;
They had something special in common, just like me and you.

And when Ben E. arrived at home that very same day;
He was so excited, he had so much to say.

His parents were sitting in the den watching Phil on T.V.
When Ben E. exclaimed proudly:
"I have a new friend, and he's ADOPTED LIKE ME."

Adoption Support & Enrichment Services

Adoption Support and Enrichment Services specializes in working with all members of "The Adoption Experience." A counseling, education and support organization, Adoption Support and Enrichment Services recognizes that adoption plays a very important role in the lives of everyone who is touched by it.

To order "Adopted Like Me"
Please send $9.95 plus $1.75 for shipping and handling to:
Jeffrey R. LaCure, M.S.W., LICSW
c/o The Adoption Advocate Publishing Company
140 David Road
Franklin, MA 02038
(508) 875-6603